SAME GENDER
loving
And Loving IT!

A guide for addressing the unique issues experienced by Black Lesbians

Love Dixon

Evolution Publishing

Dedicated to the love of my life, my wife,

Marcia Dixon.

Thank you for loving me, supporting me,

and being my HOME!

I love you.

CONTENTS

ACKNOWLEDGEMENTS

To God Be the Glory!

I am so thankful for Fran Frazier who has encouraged and supported me for many years. I can't put into words how much I value your presence in my life. Thank you for nurturing and believing in me.

I am so humbled and grateful for Cheene Richardson. I praise God everyday for bringing you into my life. You have truly saved my life. You are the wind beneath my wings!

My graphic designer Elwood Steve Berry! What would I do without you? This book would not have become a reality if you had not been in my corner. Your work is amazing and so are you!

To Stephan Wiley, the best photographer in the world and a wonderful friend. Thank you.

To my friend Marvetta Lewis, you were the catalyst to making my dream a reality. Without your sharp eye, I would still be writing this book!

JL King, Thank you for getting me on the right path and supporting me in this endeavor!

Pat Lyons, You have been a great friend and confidant for years. Your support and advice is unwavering. Thank You for your contribution to this book!

To my friends and family that have been supportive of me being Same Gender Loving, Thank you because I truly Love IT!

To my readers, always remember that YOU MATTER!

INTRODUCTION

As a 33 year old married Black lesbian, I have had to travel the same dreadful road as those that have come before me. It was a road of rejection, shame, fear, doubt, and loneliness. Not only was my voice not being heard, there were not that many voices that I could listen to that represented my struggle. Being a Black lesbian in a family that is Christian and within a community that was completely homophobic, I had to find my way in order to be healthy and happy. Like many, I hid my lesbianism, denied my lesbianism, and ran away from my lesbianism. I would have given anything if I could have just loved my ex-boyfriend the way I love my wife. I tried really hard not to be a lesbian, but it was to no avail.

After attending a church service one Sunday afternoon, I felt like my situation was hopeless. I had spent my 29th birthday at Red Lobster with a guy I barely knew and church family that I desperately wanted to accept me. After my tears burned through my pillows and my voice rang throughout my apartment from despair, I fell on my knees and began to pray. I screamed from the depth of my soul for God to change me. I wanted to be delivered from my tumultuous "sin". I promised to go and be with my ex-boyfriend and love him if God would just take the "gay" away. I wept and cried until I heard a voice say, "Child, you are perfect just the way you are and I will not change you." The voice continued and said, "I just want you to be happy. You deserve to be happy. Now go to bed and when you wake up you'll be okay."

It was 3:30am, November 13th, 2006. I woke up and was not clear if what I heard and felt was real, but I did feel better. I spent the next year processing with a therapist and healing my childhood wounds. A year later, I had clarity about who I was and who I was meant to be. I continued to attend church services and felt closer to God than ever before. I "came out" to everyone and I was ready to accept and share that I was Same Gender Loving and I was Loving "IT"!

Loving who you are and learning to be gentle with yourself is a gift. Most people spend their entire lives trying to get to the place in their life where they are comfortable with themselves. It is not easy being comfortable in your own skin when it is contrary to what society says you should be. It is not easy believing that you are wonderfully made when your religious community compares who you are to a pedophile. It is not easy standing up for who you are when your voice has been silenced by your family, your faith community, and the society in which you live. How can you thrive in a world that insists that you are a curse, a fraud, and a mistake? As a Black lesbian, you are faced with many obstacles and challenges that can sometimes impede your progress of growth, health and happiness. No matter how old you are it may be difficult to stand with pride, strength and resilience.

As a Black lesbian, situations occur often that make me uncomfortable. Although I am an out and proud lesbian, I am still put in situations where I need to come out. Every time I get a new job, meet a new person, mentor an inquisitive child, conduct a television interview, or blog, I am taking the chance of being confronted because someone didn't know I was a lesbian. My strongest reactions come from my own community, the Black community. And sometimes they are ugly monsters that spew ignorance and hate in the name of their religion.

I don't always feel like defending myself, or saying, "Yes, I am Same Gender Loving and Loving "IT". I don't always feel like having a conversation about who I am and the Lesbian, Gay, Bi-Sexual, Trans Gendered and Queer (LGBTQ) community. I don't always feel like watching what and how I say things so that the situation won't escalate. I don't always feel like participating in meaningless conversation about what the bible says or doesn't say about homosexuality. Sometimes, I just want to be left alone to just be who I am.

I know that many of you can relate. Even if you are not same gender loving, I am sure that there are people in your life that are thorns in your side because you are not who they think you should be. You don't dress the right way, act the right way, have the right hairstyle, have the right job, have the right spouse, or live in the right house or city. You may have too many children or not enough children, and so on. People are so judgmental and truly believe that their way of living is the "only right way." People believe that their path in life must be your path and they spend their energy trying to convince you that you must change by beating you with guilt and shame.

But when you know that you matter, you learn how to stand up for who you are. It truly is better to be hated for who you are than loved for who you are not. You will never be enough for the critics around you. You will never be what they want you to be. You can only be who you are. When you can accept who you are and stand up for who you are, your road to happiness will become more attainable. You can stand up for yourself, by never lying or hiding who you are to make others more comfortable. You can stand up by using your voice when given the opportunity; you can stand up by refusing to be around people that treat you bad, you can stand up by allowing the best of you to shine in every situation. No matter whom you are and how you like to express yourself, be the best! It is worth standing strong and representing your true self. You can stand for who you really are!

This may be hard for you to grasp if you are used to hiding, ducking, and lying about your reality. You may be same gender loving, but have yet to evolve to truly loving "IT". There are many people that are in this same predicament.

As I witness the hurt and pain of so many of you who are Black and same gender loving, I wonder if you have any idea the value of your existence. So many people focus on your sexuality that you forget that you are more. You allow a society that is full of hate to reduce you to a person that has "deviant" sexual desires, and you believe them to be right. You spend your days and nights praying to be different, praying that God will change you, praying that no one will figure out who you really are. You deny yourself the gift of life and the gifts that have been placed inside of you.

You are not a curse! If you were not supposed to be here, then why are there so many people across every culture, in every country that are just like you? You are a Gift! And if you would take the time to reflect on how you make our world better, happier, and more colorful, you will be able to stand proud and tall in front of your haters. People hate on you because they are envious of just how special, gifted, and talented you are. Without same gender loving people, music would be so boring. Church folks wouldn't have any songs to sing people to the altar! There would not be great hair styles, wonderful clothes, and artistic expression. Without you, there would not be so many people that are readily available to care for all of our abandoned children. Without you, our world would be so plain and boring. And the reality is the universe needs you! You spice up the world and you are not a mistake!

Mean, hateful people are illogical and usually sound like ignorant people that are sad and miserable in their own life. When you buy their opinion, you buy their lifestyle. I know that you don't want to be miserable like them! When you know that you matter, you will stand up for your own self worth! You will know that without you, the world would be dramatically different. The Black community would not function well without you. So stop letting them intimidate and change you. Remember that the same bible that they use to send you to Hell is the same bible that was used to enslave and keep them in Hell. They are only doing what was done to them. So forgive them, for they know not what they do. Keep living, keep striving, and keep being the great person that you are!

This book is designed to be the voice and guide for a community that is often left silenced in their own despair. It is intended to provide clarity as I have learned it so that Black lesbians can stand up and be proud of who they are while accepting who they are not. "Same Gender Loving and Loving It" is a tool for the Black lesbian community that offers stories of hope and love from individuals that have walked your same path. It provides insights and solutions for Black lesbian issues as it relates to the Black family/community, youth, health, relationships, and religious organizations.

I hope that while you are on your journey of life you reach a point of Loving "IT"!

CHAPTER 1

LESBIANISM

The "IT" Factor

Black lesbians are "IT"! Smart, Wonderful, Beautiful, Strong, Courageous, Valuable, Gifted, and Powerful! You are filled with passion and fire. Steam rolls off of your body as you flow through the world. Your very existence is a revolutionary act. You are free to be yourself without restraint and conformity to how the world has defined the term 'woman'. You are a breath of fresh air, breeding new thought and life. Your love is a sweet melody blooming through the soil and dirt of life. You are a gift of sunlight, shining so bright for the world to see. You are "IT"!

Loving "IT" means loving the lesbian experience, loving women and loving the life that you have been given. When you truly understand and embrace "IT", you will embrace the best of yourself. The echoes of shame, guilt, and hate will fade away when you become comfortable with loving "IT".

Loving "IT" is your birth mark on this world. It is the symbol of your tenacity to be happy and survive the negative influences of society. Being "IT" is the muscle that will move our nation forward to acceptance, peace and love. Statistics show that there are a lot of women loving "IT". You are not the only one!

Demographics of Lesbians

If you are a lesbian, a true Black lesbian, it is important that you clearly define yourself as a Black lesbian. Make sure that the priorities and perspectives of Black lesbians are represented in society based on what you believe and the lifestyle that you've chosen. Be prepared to also make a mark in society with your new found clarity. As Black lesbians we spend so much time allowing others to define who we are, how we feel, how we think, and how we are supposed to act, that we stand disillusioned as well as fretful of our very own lesbian existence.

You are a wonderful, special person. Be assured there are a lot of people just like you. You are in families, churches, schools, public and private workforces, the entertainment industry, and the fashion industry. You are even part of social societies that embrace you, but might shun your very existence if they knew who you really are. You are EVERYWHERE!

The Zuna Institute conducted research on Black lesbians called the National Black Lesbian Need Assessment. They surveyed 1,596 Black lesbians between the ages of 18 to70 in 2010. Their research found lesbianism exists with at most 37.8% of the women whom are from the southern region of the United States, which is ironic because the southern states are notoriously known for their religion and strong spiritual convictions as well as deep beliefs, followed by 29.8% from the West , 18% from the Midwest and 14.4% from the North East .

According to this survey 69.5% of the women have children or are planning to have children, 27.8% had experienced same-sex intimate partner violence, 55% were in their middle years with middle class values and viewpoints. Additionally, 84.4% completed at least a bachelor's degree. This research has opened the doors for dialogue about us and for us. As a Black lesbian you must go to the table, sit there, and let your voice be heard. This survey proves that your voice and choice is being monitored.

You Matter! And knowing that you are an intricate part of our culture, society, and country births the importance of your very existence. There is a Black lesbian represented in every major arena in our society. And guess what? You add to the beautiful fabric of our quilt.

Is it a Phase or Are You a Lesbian?

You like her. She looks good. You want her. You saw the picture on the cover of this book and thought, "This is me." But is it? Are you really a lesbian? Lesbianism is more than having a rendezvous or a threesome with your boyfriend and a girl you picked up in a club. It is more than lusting after that girlfriend that sat and talked to you for hours when her boyfriend cheated. It is more than having casual sex so that you don't have to worry about pregnancy or disease. Yes, being a lesbian is more than fruitless encounters that lead to confusion, doubt, and denial.

A lesbian is not about what you do, it's who you are. You are not a lesbian just because you have had or desire to have sex with another woman. You are a lesbian if you are a woman that desires to have serious love relationships with and/or live your life with another woman as your partner. Unless or until you determine that the above phrase describes you, you are not a lesbian.

While you are trying to figure it out, remember that senseless acts and encounters can destroy your inner soul. Not to mention, these senseless acts have the potential to create tension and uncertainty with your loved ones that surround you. Senseless acts can be a tool for total destruction of you mentally and physically. So, GET CLEAR and BE CLEAR about who you are.

Evidence That You ARE NOT a Lesbian

It is very important that the lesbian community is defined. There are so many people that act as if they represent the lesbian community because of their behaviors and desires. This causes problems and mishaps when people begin to form relationships and bonds with other women. Sometimes women are truly confused about their sexuality and because the Black community does not allow women to explore and talk about their sexuality without the fear of being disowned, many women just tread to find their way.

If you wake up in the morning and all you think about is that good looking man you saw the other day and how you would like to see him again, you ARE NOT a lesbian. If you find physical comfort in a woman that has shown you compassion, after you've been disappointed by a man in your life, you ARE NOT a lesbian. If you drifted into a same gender relationship because it was convenient at a certain time in your life, and you continue to try to mold your female partner into a "manly" woman, you ARE NOT a lesbian.

Phases and experimentation do exist. You don't have to succumb to pressures of being something that you are not just because you had a sexual encounter with a woman. Not even if you had a relationship with a woman. A lesbian is a woman that has serious love relationships and/or lives her life with another woman. Thus, if you cannot see yourself as never dating another man, never having sex with another man, or never being in relationship with a man again, you ARE NOT a lesbian.

Coming to Terms With Who You Are

So if you've determined that you are a lesbian, prepare and empower yourself. You are going to face resistance. You must be able to stand strong in your identity no matter what your friends or family say or do to shake your confidence. Go get a journal and write down everything about yourself that makes you smile. Write down how you affect and influence those around you. Think about the gifts you have to offer. Write down how your world, the world of your friends and family would be if you weren't in it. Take your time, and with deep introspection write why you matter to you.

Self esteem is built with accomplishment and a sense of self worth. You have to find out why you are important and worthy of being alive. Learn to be okay with the word lesbian. Surround yourself with positive people that build on your self esteem and provide a nurturing, stable mental environment in order for you to grow as a Black lesbian. Saying I am a beautiful lesbian every morning allows you to accept you. Pick a position and stick to it. If you are a lesbian or you have been thinking that you may be a lesbian, start becoming comfortable with yourself. It is important because before anyone will accept and love you, you have to accept and love yourself. And people can spot a fake.

To be proud, happy and Loving "IT" will take time. But remember there are thousands of Black lesbians that arrived at a place of self love, respect, and most importantly acceptance. If you are beginning your journey of truth, keep going. Stand tall and keep searching for your truth. Live it out and muster up all the strength you can find inside to allow your heart to smile. If you have been on this journey for a while, stay brave. Every opportunity you have, try to share your authentic self. People may not be interested in the real you because they have a tendency to try to make you be what they want you to be. But you will feel better about yourself when you share who you really are. Trust me. Besides, a Black lesbian might need to know they are not alone. Your true self may be just what someone else needs to take their first brave step. And for those of you who are just curious, have family members who are lesbian or just want to know if someone is really a lesbian, just listen and believe them when they tell you they are. Their actions, words, or silence will tell all.

CHAPTER 2

NO MORE SHAME

I'm Staying In

"**I**'m OUT and I'm PROUD!" Those are words that are extremely hard for Black lesbians to feel and say over and over again. Have you ever wondered why the coming out process is so difficult? Have you come out and then wanted to go back in during certain situations? Are you tired of having to "come out" every time you meet a potential new friend or colleague? Well, it's a no-brainer why you would want to stay in the closet. Coming out is not easy, and who you are is always an issue for someone, somewhere in your life. You may have days where you just don't feel like coming out and you don't feel like being messed with. If someone says the wrong thing that just might be the day that you lose it … enough said!

Staying in the closet is about you keeping the secret that you are same gender loving. For the most part, when a person keeps something a secret, they are keeping it a secret because they are ashamed of it. This shame may be conscious or unconscious. Most people do not admit to themselves "I have shame about being same gender loving." What they do is say: "I'm going to keep this to myself because I will have negative consequences if I don't, and I'm not ready for those negative consequences."

I am here to tell you it is not your fault. You are not a weak person. You are not a punk. What you are is programmed. You have received messages about the undesirability of LGBTQ people from the time you were a child. Shame was embedded in your mind before you even knew that you were a lesbian. The Black church, the Black family, and the Black community have made it a point to degrade and disrespect the LGBTQ community. You have heard them say things like:

"Um, that boy is funny", or "He has sugar in his tank", both said showing an exaggerated limp wrist.

Or you've heard, "Stop acting like a boy and go and put a dress on."

"When are you going to get a boyfriend?"

"You need to act like a lady."

"Stop cutting your hair off!"

"Why are you always hanging with that girl?"

"Something ain't right."

"People are going to start talking…"

The comments and questions about you and other people like you, imprinted on your brain that being a lesbian is not okay. I believe the Black community actually created "don't ask, don't tell." This became evident as the religious leaders allowed lesbians and gays to sing in their choir, play in their bands and lead every art program as long as they never spoke the words, "I am a homosexual." As a result, shame has become part of the identity of Black lesbians. And the Black community is the nemesis to every Black lesbian trying to live their truth.

The Black Church

The Black Church, contingent on how strong a leader is within that organization, will determine the mindset of its flock. In the Black Church the followers take what is said literally. In most cases lesbianism is not accepted. It does not matter if lesbian members have been productive, tithing members for numerous years. The Black Church will take your money, and sing your songs, but they will not acknowledge that being Christ-like and same gender loving can exist in the same person at the same time. If your own religious affiliates won't show you love and accept you for who you are, how can you ever love and accept yourself? You can start to hate yourself because your religious leaders have made you think that God hates you. You can start to think of yourself as flawed because your religious leaders have said you can be gay and not act on it. The Black Church stands at the heart of so many because of the historical past, survival of slavery and culture of the community. Many people believe every word that comes from the pulpit and will stand by what religious leaders say without even researching it. The Black Church is what has shaped your community and given you the strength to withstand all of the suffering and pain that has been endured.

As a Black lesbian, you may have grown up around the Black Church and/or other religious organizations such as Islam. You may have learned oppressive theology and began to shape your whole life on the notion that Hell is real. Of course, you wouldn't want to go to that place! The church has effectively broken the spirits of Black lesbians and often times forced many of you to marry men and create a façade life. Living a façade can have detrimental consequences for you, your children, and your faith. Because members of Black churches are taught to have faith and not question, it never enters your mind that they could be completely wrong about God, and your place in this world. The hypocritical behavior of the Black Church says, "you can't love freely here, but you can give 10% of your gross income to make sure the pastor lives in a glamorous house and drives a fabulous car."

The Black Church says, "you can't enter the Kingdom of God if you are a lesbian." But the church will allow you to compose and sing gospel songs that are vital to their worship.

The Black Church says, "We love you, but hate the sin." But some are judgmental, mean, and hateful every time they see you "acting like" a lesbian.

Because you have been taught to not ask questions, you forget that the Black Church is not God. God, or whatever higher power you choose, is Love and Love is all there is. You will not, simply cannot, go to Hell for being the person you were created to be. You were perfectly made in the image and likeness of the Creator. You can't pray away the gay. You can't 'cast out' the lesbian demon. There is no demon! Nor can you rid yourself of a feeling by dating, having sex with, marrying or having a baby with a man. The more you try to pray away the gay, the more you allow shame and guilt to ruin and run your life and your choices. Stop It! This hateful chain is why so many of you keep your secret and stay in the closet.

How to Combat Oppressive Doctrine

Go to the source. Have your own conversation with God. Get clear for yourself why you believe what you believe.

Question and don't be afraid to challenge who put those beliefs in your mind. Take time everyday to strengthen your relationship with yourself and your God. You can do this by experiencing the Creator when you go for a walk and look up to the sun smelling the aroma of the flowers blowing in the wind. You can do this by paying attention to the silence. Just listen. Listen very carefully.

You can experience the Creator by tasting the delicious food prepared by an outstanding chef or prepared by you. You can experience the Creator by watching that sports event you had been waiting to see or that great movie that made you laugh. You can experience a higher power by experiencing life every day, thus making sure that you do enough things that put a smile in your heart. God is not only in the church. You don't have to live by dogma rules to know and feel God. You can love God just where you are. You can experience God and be a Black lesbian.

Explore other venues. There are many churches that are loving and affirming. The United Church of Christ and many non-denominational churches are accepting of you. You can always go and build yourself up with knowledge and the truth as it relates to the Bible. Many religious leaders of open and affirming churches will teach on the "clobber" scriptures that Christians use to kill the spirit of homosexuals. Get educated so that you can feel good about what the Creator actually says about you. There are many books and resources that provide clarity and understanding about the "clobber" scriptures. I suggest "What the Bible Really Says About Homosexuality" by Daniel Helminiak. This is a great book to start your own research about the matter.

If you are not a Christian, but affiliated with another religion there are groups that support lesbians and would accept you without question as you try to be in worship with your Creator. Buddhism and Hinduism are two such religions.

Staying in the closet for whatever reason will induce a spiritual suicide process. You will be more like a dead woman walking than a purposeful lesbian being. And you were created for a purpose. There is no life in lying, hiding, and pretending while staying within religious walls that someone else built. By staying in, and contained, you let your religious leaders believe that they are right. You perpetuate the shame they put on you every time you deny who you know you really are. As a Black lesbian, you must let the shame go so that you can move forward with your goals, aspirations, and life.

The Black Family

Have you ever wanted to go out somewhere with your lover or partner, yet couldn't because of who else might be there and what information might get back to your family members? Have you ever chosen your outfit and styled your hair in a way so that your family wouldn't think you look like a lesbian? Have you ever referred to the love of your life as your "friend" or allowed your family to do so? Have you ever spent holidays away from your lover because you knew it would be awkward or difficult to take her home to your family? Have your family members ever popped up at your home unexpectedly and you had to pretend that your girlfriend is your BFF or business associate? Have you ever been told by anyone in your family, "I don't care what you do in private, but don't throw it up in my face?" If you answered yes to any of these questions, you have felt the same fear that many other Black lesbians have felt; the fear of losing your family.

Family is extremely important in the Black community. Unfortunately, many Black families are not gay-friendly. Some Black families may be gay-tolerant, but if tolerance is all you can ever hope for from your family if you come out, you might think it's better to stay in the closet.

The Black woman is a monument of resilience, strength, endurance, long suffering, pain and the "everything" to everyone! This is no different among Black lesbians. You want to be that strong woman force in your family and do not want to be rejected or seen as "the deviant". You put up with your family situation because you fear losing their love, their acceptance, and everything that makes you who you are. It is the center of your being, and you feel adrift without your family connection. No matter how dysfunctional your family is you still want to be accepted by them. You want to keep them in your life and will go to immeasurable lengths to do so. So at times you may shrink and contain yourself in a mold just to hold on to whatever type or amount of love your family chooses to give. As a result you may hide, you may lie, and you may not live out your life fully. But you must understand that the hiding and the lying will make you incapable of reaching your higher potential. Staying in the closet can be safe and comfortable. But you have to realize that it is only safe and comfortable on the outside, because it is killing your inner being.

How to Deal With Your Family

The hard truth is your family is not showing you love by denying that different parts of you exist. Your family is causing you more harm than good. If you take the time to think about it, your family members are living the lives they want to live. They probably didn't consider you when they made choices about their lives and for their lives. They probably won't ask your permission to date who they want, dress how they want, and act how they want. So why do you feel the need to have their approval and acceptance to be who you are?

You have to take a firm stand for who you are. You have to consistently show your family members how to treat you. Here are some suggestions:

1. **Speak up.** Each time someone in your family refers to your lover as your "friend" say: "Mom/Dad/Auntie/Uncle/ Sis/Bro, so-and-so is not my 'friend', she is my girlfriend/

wife/partner. We are in a relationship. Please refer to her as my girlfriend/wife/partner''.

2. **Open up.** When you talk to any of your relatives, talk openly about your life. Tell them about the break-up you just had, or the wonderful woman you just met. Tell them about the volunteer work you're doing with gay and lesbian youth or the Black Pride festival you can't wait to attend. If you're in a committed relationship, tell them about the wonderful vacation you just took or about the future plans you two are excited about. Let your partner answer your phone a few times and give your relatives an opportunity to talk to this great woman you are sharing your life with.

3. **Show yourself.** If you enjoy wearing your pride rainbow accessories, wear them. If you normally dress in loose clothing, wear a hat to the back, or wear cologne, wear it. It may be difficult to hear the comments, but they'll get over it. In the meantime, you'll feel much more comfortable than you would wearing pantyhose and wobbling around in heels!

4. **Pull back from haters.** Some family situations are worse than others. If your family is disrespectful and tears you down, despite your efforts to lovingly share your full self with them, then you should not be in their presence. For instance, if your family members act as though your

girlfriend is not standing right next to you and ignore her whenever you bring her around, stop going to their get-togethers. If your family members choose to debate with you about "your lifestyle" every time you see them, stop going around them. While this tactic may be difficult at first it is a method of tough love. Your family members will see that you are serious, and they will adjust their behavior if they want you in their lives. You have to know and communicate to your family that you are a prize and they don't deserve you if they can't treat you well. Your family will always be your family. They will miss you and eventually come back to you. It may take them a while but know that it will happen.

5. **Get closer to the people that love and accept you.** Most people have at least one person in their family that is supportive of them. Start spending more time with the supportive people in your family. Maybe that cousin that always has your back, or your grandma that says she'll always love you no matter what. Also, look outside of your bloodline and search out all of the love and support available from friends. Get closer to them and draw strength from them. Create your own family of friends if you must. No one deserves to be alone. Family members that you choose can make the pain a little more bearable.

CHAPTER 3

COMING OUT/ BEING OUT

Coming out is a delicate process that is different for everyone. It should be done in your own time and in your own way. If you are not okay with who you are and if you are still waiting for the Creator to change you, then it may not be your time to come out. You have to be your own cheerleader and advocate when you make this leap. You have to believe in yourself.

You may be scared out of your mind. You may feel nervous, sick to your stomach, and anxious. But trust me when I tell you that coming out can be the most exhilarating and powerful choice you can make in your life. Coming out frees you from the inner shame and hate that you may feel. It stops your emotional suicide. You will come out when you are certain there is nothing wrong with you and you know that you are beautiful, wonderful, and exactly as you should be. Coming out allows you to express yourself without embarrassment, guilt or shame.

The Coming Out Process

1. **Come out to yourself.** It may sound weird but it must be done. Lying to yourself can be a dangerous thing. If you don't love yourself as a lesbian then there is no way you can ever get your family, your friends, or your church to accept you and respect you as a lesbian. Ask yourself questions like:

   "How long have I felt this way?"

   "Is this a phase?" If it is, that is ok.

   "Am I just mad at my boyfriend/husband?" If you are, that is ok.

   "Can I live without intimacy with a man for the rest of my life?"

   "Can I live without intimacy with a woman for the rest of my life?"

   Ask yourself every hard question you can think of and then answer the questions honestly.

Once you are sure that what you are is same gender loving, say to yourself, "I am a lesbian." Look in the mirror, smile, and say it. "I am a lesbian." Say it until it feels real, until "I" and "lesbian" feel like the same concept to your brain— You are lesbian and lesbian is you. Make sure you are ok with the word lesbian being associated with you. Your process of coming out to yourself is complete when you can say to yourself, "I am a lesbian" without any embarrassment or shame.

2. **Seek the support of a counselor or your closest, dearest friend and confidant.** Now I know that it is taboo in the Black community to talk to a psychologist or a counselor because "what happens in the family, stays in the family." This phrase is another way we are trapped in the stigma of our choices. Nonetheless, if you want to survive the cruel, cold and brutal reaction of your family, your religious leaders, and some friends, you need someone who knows and understands your issue. You need someone who can be objective and does not have a personal stake in your sexual identity. Therapy allows you to know, understand, and process your feelings, thoughts, and needs. Healthy people go to therapy! It is unhealthy people that are unwilling to examine, review, think, and change their lives. A good therapist can and will be objective and assist you in finding the answers you need to survive. A great friend and confidant will accept you no matter what. They will let you come out in your own time. They will stay on the

phone and talk with you for hours. They will give you a shoulder to snot on and lay. They will be in your corner and have your back.

3. **Come out to everyone else, in your time, in your way.** When you come out to anyone else in your life the result can be a toss-up. Be prepared. Be very prepared. You may get some reactions that are loving, gentle, caring, and sincere. This response usually comes from close friends who have been exposed to and have personal experience with people that are different than they are. You may get some reactions that are cruel and downright heartless. And where people fall among supporters and non-supporters may really surprise you. The person you think loves you the most might be the least supportive and the person you are not sure about might end up coming out to you! Just be emotionally prepared for anything.

For both supporters and non-supporters you must prepare for the great sexuality debate. Some of your friends and family will react to your coming out by trying to convince you that you have it wrong, and you are not, in fact a lesbian. If you let them, they will use everything they know about your past and any information you have told them about yourself and throw it in your face to prove that you are not really a lesbian. Your mother will say that it is just a phase and that you just need to meet a "good guy", that your sexuality is a response to a man shortage. You will be told that this is a reaction to being abused or treated poorly by men. You will be told that because you were once married to a man or had a baby with a man that you cannot possibly be a lesbian. Parents and siblings will use every high school, college, or young adult boyfriend you ever had as undeniable proof that you are not a lesbian. And you will be told that it is a choice and you can choose differently.

To combat these arguments you must prepare your own arguments and collect your own proof so that you do not waiver when confronted in this way. Be prepared to share with your friends and family information about how long you have been attracted to women. Share the difference in how attracted you were to men and how much more attracted you are to women. Share the reasons that you want to live your life with a woman. Share that you didn't come out earlier because you had some feelings of shame and fear that you needed to deal with. Let them know how certain you are that you are a lesbian. Let them know you love who you are. You have to stay strong and consistent with who you are. The arguments of your friends and family may be persistent, but you cannot let them change your identity.

There is No Right Time and There is No Perfect Way to Come Out

Now, let's be real. You will have consequences when you first come out. You may be discriminated against at work, you may be dragged through an ugly divorce, your ex-husband, ex-boyfriend, or your parents may do things to turn your children against you, and your friends might start to treat you differently. If you are already out you've discovered that you continually have to decide if you will come out in each new life situation and face the consequences that might arise. No matter how long you have been out you always have shit to deal with because negative and spiteful people exist, and you definitely know some of them. It is a difficult choice to make because only you have to live with the consequences and only you know what your consequences will be. Because you will have consequences, it is important that you come out in your own way, in your own time.

Devon, a 36 year old Black lesbian said, "I don't come out anymore. I just live. Heterosexuals don't make an announcement that they are straight!" She is a corporate executive and refuses to come out to anyone. When she is with her wife, she introduces her as her wife. She just flows with who she is and expects others to follow, respectfully of course.

You may choose the same course of action in each new situation. For instance, when you are talking to your mom and she asks if you are dating any nice men, you might say, "Oh no, I really only date women. And I'm dating one woman that I really like, her name is..." That might lead naturally into a discussion in which you can tell her more. Or she might accept your statement and roll with it. No fuss, no drama.

Gloria, a 33 year old vibrant woman, was recently married to her wife in the Midwest at a Black Church. Most people would consider her to be out. Gloria is a school teacher and has a religious leadership in her middle school. When she first started working at her school her boss, the principal, asked her not to come out to any of her co-workers. The principal feared Gloria's co-workers would not be as cooperative or friendly toward her. The principal also feared that the students and their parents would make Gloria's job difficult. When she started her job Gloria watched what she said and did careful not to share her life with most of her co-workers.

If your situation is like Gloria's, it may not be best to come out to everyone as soon as you meet them. Gloria's strategy was to get to know her co-workers and get a feel for their openness and come out to them individually as time passed. Her coming out process at work took about a year and a half, but now she is comfortable and able to fully be herself. It may work the same way for you in your workplace or in your family. Slow and steady, a little at a time. Never lie, never betray yourself, but do it at the pace that best fits your situation.

If you make the choice to come out, your bravery will lead to liberation. Every instance will be different. You can take the approach that best fits you. Coming out is a personal choice and decision because you have to deal with the effects. But no matter what you choose, coming and staying out is always, always worth it because you will be free!

Down Low Lesbian: Face Your Fears

It's not just for men. Women are on the down low everywhere. A woman that is on the down low has sexual encounters or even sexual relationships with other women while maintaining a heterosexual relationship and lifestyle with a man. Basically, a woman that is in a "real" relationship with a man but secretly sleeps with women on the side is said to be on the down low. Down low lesbians can usually hide under the radar because they don't usually have consequences like turning up with a disease or getting pregnant by accident and not knowing the identity of the father.

If you are on the down low, just stop! Stop hiding and stop using people! Your actions are not a true representation of who you really are. If you are a lesbian, being on the down low is just a cowardly way for you to have your cake and ice cream and eat it too! But, you're choking on all those goodies aren't you? You are not happy with your situation. You are consumed with fear. You are afraid that you will lose everything if you tell the truth and come out. You know what I am talking about. You remember talking with your friends and you were the one who said, "Girl, I could NEVA"! Meanwhile, you were the very one that was fantasizing about getting busy with that dime piece at your gym. You are in terror thinking, "What would happen if they knew?"

Two women, May and Debra, talked about their down low experience and how they chose to deal with it. May, a

48 year old mother of two girls, lives in Oregon with her husband. She has been married for over 25 years. For the last two years she secretly had a girlfriend while still being married. She lived a double life. She talked on the phone with her lover throughout each day. She reveled in their stolen moments and their love-making. At home she did her duty, taking care of the house, the kids, and her husband. She believed that she was in love with her girlfriend and only committed to her husband. She felt like she was caught up in a whirlwind of passion. She told her girlfriend she would leave her husband but took no real steps to make it happen.

The passion and craziness came to a boiling point when May discovered that her girlfriend was cheating on her with another lesbian. May tried desperately to "save" the relationship, but became disillusioned when her girlfriend did not seem as interested. May's emotions erupted like a volcano. May cried, "I am so in love with her. How could she keep doing me wrong?" She explained that she would lay next to her husband at night crying for her lover while he slept. She eventually told her husband about the affair but she withheld the truth about the seriousness of her relationship with her girlfriend. She confided in me that she was relieved she had not taken a leap of faith into the arms of a woman that was not "committed" to her. "I would have lost everything, for nothing."

For May, living on the down low meant she was not completely present for anyone in her life. Her body was at home with her children and her husband but her thoughts and emotions were with the woman she loved. However, she could never develop a true love relationship with the woman she loved because she could not devote the time and energy to her. She was a soul in limbo. She didn't see that her situation could have turned out better if she had not allowed her fear to paralyze her.

Debra, a 31 year old engaged mother, found herself completely attracted to females. She created an account to chat with women online. She finally connected with a woman named, Tyra, and decided to meet her for a drink. One thing led to another and the two of them began having sex on a consistent basis. But Debra had no plans of leaving her male fiancé. "I told myself I didn't need to come out because I wasn't a lesbian. I just enjoyed the sex, it was exciting. But the truth is I was really into her. I even stopped wanting sex with my man. I finally told him that I thought I may be bi-sexual because I thought it was safer. He just looked at me perplexed. Although, he made a statement that maybe we could finally have a threesome, I knew then that I needed to keep my business to myself. Just the thought of canceling my wedding and explaining it all to my parents and friends was just more than I could handle. Not to mention, coming out to my son. It's just so much easier to just go along to get along."

Down low Black lesbians are more common than you think. Integrity is important no matter who you are.

Homosexuality does not exclude you from being an honest, disciplined person. If you are not sure about your sexuality then you should sit tight and do nothing. Do not jump into a sexual relationship with a woman. Society treats Black lesbians the way we treat ourselves. They follow our lead. If you live in shame, deceit, and under false pretenses, society will never respect you as a Black lesbian. They will always think you are confused and just need a good man. Change the way you see yourself as well as the way you act.

Erase the shame forever more. There is no need for you to be living a lie in front of your children, with your friends, and your family. If you are in a relationship make it a real relationship. It can be hard, but it is so worth it!

CHAPTER 4

STEP OUT
OF YOUR ROLE

Are You the Man or the Woman?

"Who is the boy in your relationship?" I know that you have heard this question fifty million times. Yep. Heterosexuals always want to know which of you play the male role. It is one of the first questions they ask when they know you are in a relationship. It's as though they are enamored with the concept. But what they are really doing is trying to make sense of something they don't understand. Your friends and family, and even you, understand heterosexual relationships. There's a man that is supposed to be strong, in charge, sexually aggressive, and the provider for the family and there is a woman that is supposed to be supportive, nurturing, sexually submissive, and the homemaker for the family. So, when they see two women in a relationship, they try to put them into the same man/woman framework. And, because you grew up in the same society as they did, you might, unconsciously, do the same thing. There is truth in every stereotype. One of the women in your relationship might wear men's clothes, walk like a man, talk like a man because both of you think there should be a man. But the truth is that in a lesbian relationship, there is no man. Period.

Don't Put Yourself in a Box

By believing there should be "boys" and "girls" in the lesbian community, some lesbians believe they need to choose the "type" of lesbian they want to be. Examples include: aggressive, a stud, a soft-stud, a femme, a high femme, or aggressive femme. So what role have you agreed to play in the Black lesbian world? Are you a stud, believing your role is to be the alpha male at all times, walking, talking, dressing, and acting more like a man than any natural-born man around? Do you play this role even though you don't want your mother to know you are playing it? If you are playing the stud role, you might believe you cannot cry or be emotional. You might believe you must wear clothes that disguise your curves. You might believe that you must always be "on top" when you have sex. You might believe that you cannot get pregnant and give birth to a child. If you have chosen to be a Femme, you might wear makeup, skirts, and heels at times you'd rather be wearing sweats and flip flops. You might believe you must always be "on the bottom" when you have sex and that you cannot be sexually aggressive. If you are playing the femme role you might always submit to your stud, allowing her to make decisions for the both of you even in situations in which you are more informed or have the relevant experience to make the best decision. You might bite your tongue a lot, frequently stroke her ego, and do all you can to make her feel more like a "man".

When you choose to play a role, like Stud or Femme or anything in between, you put yourself in a box with one of those labels on it. Each box and label comes with a certain mindset, a type of clothing, hairstyle, walk, talk, and sexual activity. Your role as a Black lesbian becomes the epicenter of how you are identified. It is a key indicator of how you choose to express yourself, your life, and how people will view you. Often times, unknowingly, you put out what you want people to see. That, ultimately, is how those same people will perceive who you are. Humans love naming things. Any time there is a group of people that does not fit the standard and "status quo", a name is created and a box is found so they can be set apart, picked on, and secluded. The box that you put yourself in can be used to imprison you.

As a Black lesbian, do not allow anyone to label you and put you into a box and definitely don't put yourself in such a box. Stop confusing certain personality traits or characteristics with male or female attributes. If you desire to be strong, in control, confident, and smart you can be all of those things without taking on male attributes. Men do not own those characteristics. You do not have to wear men's clothes to feel like you are strong and in control. As a woman you can have a confident swagger, be in control, and be sexually aggressive. Your partner can be soft-spoken, nurturing, supportive, and sexually submissive, or vice-versa. Within either woman, any one of these characteristics can come to the surface at different times depending on the situation. The spectrum of womanhood is wide and vast, so there are many ways to be a woman. Neither of you need to see yourself or the other as "the man" or "the woman". So even though people, including your partner, might try to put you in a role or make you stay in a role, remember, you don't have to buy what they are selling. You can choose to be just you and nothing more.

Kelly, from Virginia, considers herself to be a feminine lesbian (femme). She says, "I love to indulge in my femininity." She likes shopping, cooking, cleaning, caring for her family, and being a wife. She sadly admits, "Everyone sees me as a soft stud because of how I dress." Kelly hates that she is believed to be something she is not just because of her choice of clothing. She is a tomboy who loves to play and watch sports and most of the time she prefers to be comfortable rather than sexy. She enjoys putting on her high heels, make-up, tight jeans and skirts when she is going out on the town with her wife. But on any given day you can find her in a t-shirt, jeans or sweats. Despite feeling the pressure to fit into a role Kelly has mastered the art of simply being herself.

Stephanie likes to tease society. She oozes feminine sexuality and overturns people's expectations of what she should look like. She will dress very feminine at times and the next day she may dress like a complete stud. She recently cut all of her hair off just because she felt like it. She does not prescribe to the labels of society. She simply says, "I am a woman and I love it"!

What if Labels Work For You?

I understand that you might be perfectly comfortable and happy with the role you are playing. You might feel that having a "man" and a "woman" in a lesbian relationship works well for you because it creates balance and assists you in finding a mate that will be compatible. As a stud, you might feel invincible when you stroll down the street in your fly suit with your woman on your arm. As a femme you might get really turned on when you see your muscular woman coming your way sporting a fresh haircut and smelling of that great cologne you gave her. If this is your story then rock on! Do what works for you. But, please, make sure it actually does work for you and it works for your partner.

Make sure it is your choice. Loving who you are as a Black lesbian means loving all of you. You cannot love all of you if you feel constrained and you are not free to express every aspect of your personality, cannot display all of your skills and talents, or cannot express your full range of emotions.

Also, keep in mind that gender identity is completely different than sexual orientation. If you find yourself wishing you were man, using a male name, or sometimes referring to yourself as a man, you do not have an issue with role playing, but with gender identity. I do not discuss gender identity here, but there are resources available to you if you believe that you struggle with gender identity.

No matter how you dress or what you call yourself, as a Black lesbian you are a woman, and being a woman is wonderful! Lets show society that there are infinite ways to be a woman. They need to get a clue! Embrace who you are. Embrace being same gender loving and that will lead to Loving IT.

CHAPTER 5

THE IMPORTANCE OF BEING HEALTHY

"Hurt People, hurt people!" I know you have heard this saying before. And there is truth in it! Take a moment and think about all the people in your life that have hurt you. If you look closely, you will find that before they hurt you, they were in pain themselves. When people are hurting, they give themselves permission to hurt others. The problem is until they deal with their hurt, they will continue to spread hurt among all who cross their path. This cycle causes distress on every human being walking this earth. You have to break this cycle by dealing with the hurt in your life. You have a responsibility to yourself to heal from your past and present pain. In order to be healthy you must take a look at the things that ail you in your life.

As I watch the news, the one constant in every crime and act of violence committed is that the perpetrators are in pain and hurting. They are wrapped up in their own unresolved hurt. It is important that you are aware of all ways that being unhealthy can affect your life. Emotional, mental, and physical health play a large role in you being your highest self and living your best life. Mental illness, obesity, drug and alcohol abuse, and emotional illness are plaguing our country and Black lesbians are not exempt. You have to look good on the outside and feel good on the inside in order to love "IT".

Now, don't get brand new on me. I know you have seen Black lesbians that are mentally ill, out of shape, overweight, sound strange, act crazy, and look a hot mess. You know them. They live in your city. They go to your church. They are marching in the pride parade. They are trying to date you. They are everywhere except at the therapist's office and the gym. It's almost as if they feel like they don't need to keep themselves up because they are not with a man. It's like the pressures of being a woman in today's society is lifted because they are lesbian. Well it's not! As a Black lesbian you still have to feel good emotionally and look good even if only for yourself.

Self-destructive behaviors such as overeating, under-exercising, promiscuity, and drug and alcohol abuse exist among Black lesbians. The reasons for self-destruction stem from trauma, shame, guilt, and pressures that you face as a Black lesbian.

Emotional Health

You are a woman! Your emotions fly high at least for a week every month. Other times your passion can consume you and cause you to be a little off balance. It is in your DNA. So it is important that you take the necessary steps to keep your emotions in check.

Take breaks. Everyone needs breaks sometimes. You may need a break from work, from your children, from your friends and family and from your intimate partner. You may need a break from the negative thoughts and influences in your life. You may need a break from your religion. You may need a break from yourself!

Breaks are necessary and important during your journey. Your emotional health relies on breaks to keep you balanced. It is during the breaks when you are rejuvenated and renewed. It is your time to relax and refocus on what is important in your life. Life has a way of beating you down and at times you can get sick of life and everything in it. It is during those times when you need to learn to be gentle with yourself. You will learn that you are doing the best you can with what you have and it is okay to make mistakes and take a break from it all. To err is human. Emotions are healthy and natural. And breaks are a gift that keeps on giving.

Feel your feelings. Your feelings are valuable and deserve to be felt. Give yourself permission to feel the feelings that flow through you because stuffing them down can erupt and be explosive to those around you. As a Black lesbian it is important to allow yourself to feel the anger from being an outcast and marginalized. When you feel the anger, it will polarize and lose its power so that you can move through it and move on.

All emotions work the same way. Once you feel the feeling and experience it, you are free to move on. Many people waste their energy trying to not feel their feelings. They say things like "I shouldn't even be mad...I knew what I was getting into." What is the point of such a statement? There is no point. It is a waste of time because you will eventually feel that anger you are trying to talk yourself out of feeling. All you are doing is delaying the experience. You don't need to be in the perfect place and it doesn't need to be the perfect time for you to feel your feelings. You can feel them for as long as it takes for you to move on. I keep stressing moving on because emotions can keep you stuck in despair. Emotions can have you miss some of the beautiful experiences of life. Emotions can land you in jail, or stir up a war in your life. So be careful and allow yourself to feel. Let the toxins out and breathe in life. You are worth "IT".

Mental Health

Mental health is vital to the well being of Black lesbians. Although it is a sensitive topic for the Black community, it is necessary that an honest, open dialogue occurs so that healing can take place. There are several causes to mental illness. Some illnesses are heredity and some are caused by environments and trauma. Many Black lesbians have suffered childhood and adulthood trauma. This has led to a community of women that suffers from depression, suicidal tendencies, bipolar disorder, post traumatic stress syndrome, drug and alcohol abuse, and much more. There are also so many lesbians that have internalized homophobia. This stops you from loving who you really are as well. In order to get to a place of loving "IT", you must first love "YOU". It is extremely hard to grow into a healthy adult and have the life that you desire if you have not dealt with the issues that keep your mind tangled up in fragmented pieces.

According to the Zuna Institute research, Black lesbians are less likely to seek out traditional professional mental help than are their white counterparts, even when combating grave mental health concerns. For example, there is a pattern of higher suicide rates among Black lesbians and particularly higher rates among those from economically disenfranchised communities. Zuna Institute concluded that scholars have primarily associated these higher suicide rates with one's inability to deal with 'coming out' and the social constructions of the 'strong Black woman'.

Being a 'strong Black woman' can lead to family secrets, silenced voices, denial, mistrust, and loneliness. I in 4 women have been sexually abused or assaulted in America. Chances are you or someone you know is going through pain and agony as a result of sexual abuse. So how does being a 'strong Black woman' make you equipped to deal with everything that comes your way? Actually, it doesn't! Trauma of any type can make the strongest crumble. As a Black lesbian, you have to deal with your trauma and being a lesbian simultaneously. This can be unbearable at times and require extra attention and help for your survival.

Life can be so unpredictable. Without any cause on your part, life can hand you a bottomless pit of hurt, pain, and misery. Sometimes all you have to do is breathe and storms will fall down on your life. Some of you have been through experiences that are so painful that you are now empty and hopeless. Trauma feels the same no matter who is experiencing it and at times can make your life intolerable.

When I was 8 years old, I experienced unbearable trauma. I was left alone to deal with the invasion of my body by an adult male that was in my life. I felt betrayed and I had to fight with all my might to become healthy and okay with my existence. Some people wonder how I am so successful and happy after all that I have been through. My answer is simply four words: God, love, hope, and resiliency. I believed that I could be happy and I never stopped trying until I became happy. I realized that it was no longer my job to punish my mother or care about the decisions that she made or did not make in her life. My only job was to become happy. Resiliency is the gift that you have in your corner after a traumatic event.

When you are trying to survive and become healthy, writing in journals, therapy, having a network of friends/ mentors, scrap booking, setting future goals, reading books of empowerment, joining groups or clubs that give you hope, and using your artistic gifts, are all things that will lead to resiliency.

You must first take off the "strong black woman" mask that you wear everyday and allow yourself to admit when you feel overwhelmed or when you are hurting. Love yourself enough to get the help that you need. Trauma and mental illness can cause problems and complications in your life. Not dealing with your 'stuff' can keep you locked up in your own internal prison and stop you from enjoying your life.

"I have been through the storm of life, most of my life. My cries rang out so loud and thunderous, but no one heard them. I struggled with life and hated living each day. My suicide attempts were to no avail and I was left with the turmoil and pain that was imbedded in my soul. I tried to keep it in my family, but my family betrayed me, left me, and denied me. And so with my last attempt at life, I entered into an intensive therapeutic program. I learned how to love myself, love others, and live." —Tonya from Ohio.

What is happening in your life that you are tired of being silent about because it is killing you? What pain, abuse or oppression are you hiding from the world? What are you allowing to keep you stagnant and in fear? You can only be silent for so long. The silence will destroy you, or will erupt out of your soul like a volcano. At some point in your life, you have to speak out against the suffering that you endure. There comes a time when you have to use your voice to empower yourself and let the dirty little secrets out. Release yourself from turmoil and the hell that you have been living.

When you stay silent, you give people permission to keep hurting you and others. Exposing the atrocities that occur is the only way to stop them. The country is learning this lesson, history has taught this lesson, and the rest of the world is starting to believe in this lesson. So must you! Take your power back by being silent NO More!!!

Like Tonya and me, you can be happy and overcome the mental illness that you suffer. The road ahead can be excruciating but therapy can be the answer to your prayers. It can uplift you and help you to change how you think about yourself and what messages you give yourself daily. Of course you should be cautious when seeking therapy. Not all therapists are good therapists. Conversely not all therapists understand your mental issues. Interview therapists before you divulge all of your information. Find out as much about a potential therapist as you possibly can. Knowing as much as you can about them will assure that you have found someone that is a right fit for you. If mental health insurance coverage is an issue for you, then seek out help at the local mental health agency in your city. Such agencies often provide individual and group counseling for no cost or at a price based on your income.

Physical Health

In a report entitled "Health Issues of Aging African American Lesbians" Crawford, Dribble, and Nussy found that "Black lesbians were more likely to have no regular source for medical care, be uninsured, be overweight/ obese, be a current smoker, drink more than 3 drinks per drinking day, and take medication when diagnosed with hypertension." They also found that Black lesbians have shorter life expectancies, higher death rates from heart disease, diabetes, and cerebrovascular disease, lower levels of physical activity, higher levels of dietary fat consumption, and fewer daily servings of fruits and vegetables. Factor in an astronomically high suicide rate and Black lesbians are certainly at a deficit when it comes to physical health and wellness.

Are you thinking, "Damn, that can't be me?" Well I'm thinking "That can't be us!" You matter. You are the only one that can change these negative factors about you and our community. I am not saying you should succumb to the pressure most women feel to be a size 6 or smaller. I am just saying that if you want to love your life you have to feel your best! You have to take care of your body. This is something you can control. No one made you overweight but you so, it's also on you to change it. If your economic situation stops you from getting fit via a gym membership, there are other affordable options and things you can do.

Black lesbians have several challenges to getting fit. You have stressors upon stressors that exhaust you and take away your energy. You have work, school, kids, relationship drama, and family drama. If you had the energy, you probably wouldn't have the time to fit in a workout. But you CAN stop the cycle of obesity. Taking care of your physical self will prevent you from beating up yourself and your self esteem.

So get to the gym and work out at least an hour a day. Listen to some music and use that as your "me" time. Walk a little more each day. Adventure past the threshold of your home, get to know your neighborhood, and experience nature at your local parks and recreation facilities. You can walk up and down the steps in your home for an hour while holding a can of collard greens in each hand. Do sit-ups and push-ups through every commercial break when you are watching TV. Get it in girl! Make a vow to yourself that when you have the choice to move, you will.

Purge your cupboards of all the sugar, high fat, and toxic items. Reduce unhealthy foods in your life. Eat more vegetables, whole grains, and fruits. Drink more water. Take stress walks at work. Keep clear of people that you know are bringing the stress and negative energy.

Get up and get busy getting healthier! You don't have to die. You don't deserve to die. Prepare yourself for what is to come in your life. Get it together. You deserve to be the best you. You are a strong Black lesbian and being strong really means seeking help and having the audacity to become happy! You can love "IT"; you can love You!

CHAPTER 6

RELATIONSHIPS

"I wake up in the morning and taste the desire to have someone next to me to hold. I penetrate my thoughts, focusing on the one that will gaze my soul. I am longing for love..."

I wonder if most people feel like the lines above. I wonder if the fabric of their being can't be made whole unless they have intimate love in their life. I wonder if knowing that you matter is contingent on who is in your life and who loves you. I wonder why having love is so important.

Longing for something that is an innate desire must be like a person held captive that wants to breathe in the fresh air and feel the sunlight on their face. Love is the beat of the heart that creates rhythm in your life. I get why you want love. I get why you need love.

I too longed for love in my life. Everybody just wants to be loved. But what I realized is that there was work to be done on myself before I could have another love me. I had to turn that longing on the inside first and become my first love. To have love you have to grow in love with yourself over and over again.

I hope you long to be in love with yourself. Someone will be attracted to your light and come your way! As I think about myself, this is what I have to say...

"The softness of my touch caressed my face and glowed as my smile ignited the room. I am like a flower that was potted and planted with care, waiting for my time to bloom. My hair is as strong as an ox, beautifully shining its power and strength. My mind is steeped in greatness, entangled with my heart which is all love and courage. I am the song of life that has persevered through it all. I am one with God because I am Love." So before you go out looking for a relationship, what do you have to say about yourself?

You can get a relationship, that's easy. If you don't want a messed up, hectic, unloving, unfulfilled relationship, you have to do some work. There is a process that you have to go through to have a healthy relationship. As a lesbian your relationship can be more complicated than the heterosexual relationships of those around you. It is important that you are as emotionally and mentally healthy as you can be before you entertain merging your life with someone else, especially if that someone else is a woman. The emotions of women can make both of you crazy at times. High emotions can create an unbalance in lesbian relationships and, if you are not careful, some serious damage can be done.

10 Steps to a Healthy Relationship

1. Get clear about who you are!

Before you jump between the sheets and U-haul into the house of the one you just met two weeks ago, get into you! There is nothing worse than when you meet someone, have sex with them, and almost immediately, you think you two are ready to play 'house'. It's just not acceptable. Just in case you have never heard of U-hauling, it is when you take all your baggage, move in with someone you just met and act like you are in love just because you had good sex! Better stated, you U-hauled your butt into an unhealthy house and relationship along with your excess baggage. This behavior is killing Black lesbian relationships and it makes us look silly to the rest of society. The image that we portray says that we are not serious about our lives, our relationships, or our love.

Getting into you involves treating yourself very, very well. It involves wining and dining yourself. Healthy relationships require healthy individuals that have their shit together, know what they want in life, and are actively going after getting what they want.

Have you ever lived alone? Do you know what you like, what you can do without, and what makes you happy? Have you written your goals and dreams down and framed them? Do you know how you are going to accomplish them? Have you worked on your issues, childhood stuff, past relationships that broke your heart and emptied out all that baggage? Are you financially stable? Do you have a job, a career? Are you secure with who you are, with whom you've become? Are you clear about your spiritual beliefs? Are you prepared to challenge what you've come to believe as the absolute gospel? Are you clear about what is important to you? Do you have children? Do you want children? Have you told your children you are a lesbian? Do you love you, really love YOU? Before you begin seeking, or perhaps begging for a relationship, answer those critical questions. Start thinking critically about yourself. Figure yourself out first! Bringing people into your messy life will create two messy lives. You will love your life if you start out by loving you.

Karen, from Texas, was in a relationship with a woman when she was 20 years old. She hadn't taken the time to really get into herself, explore her options of who she was. She had major issues that plagued her. Her girlfriend, Anne, was older, more settled, and completely "out" with her family and friends and more importantly with herself. Anne was very comfortable with being a lesbian. Karen, however, was in denial and thought that being with a woman was just a phase at this stage in her life. Besides, she thought, she was young and had time to get out and over this hump. She denied her sexuality, her wants, and desires. Whenever her family asked about it or Anne, she called Anne her "best friend" and her "roommate". She cleverly shrugged off the idea that she and Anne were an item.

It didn't matter that she was madly in love with Anne. She hated herself for being in denial with her family and more importantly for lying about Anne. This behavior therefore caused irredeemable harm to her self-esteem and relationship. Their relationship became a lie that was unbearable and miserable. Anne gave her an ultimatum to either come out and be true to herself or get out of the relationship. Ultimately, she got out. Karen was a hot ass mess. She didn't know what to do with herself and her life. She didn't know how to accept her choice to be lesbian and be comfortable enough with herself to be truthful with her family. Her fear and past issues kept her deeply angry as if a tornado raged inside her soul daily. By the time she decided to come out the experience was nothing like she'd imagined. She remembers saying to herself, "I lost everything, my dignity, my respect, my soul. My parents didn't trip on me like I thought they would, nonetheless, I lost love, the true love of my life."

Karen, like many Black lesbians, believed that she could create a healthy relationship despite the fact that she had not dealt with her fear and shame related to being a lesbian. She couldn't!

2. Value yourself

If I offered you food I got out of a dumpster, you would be insulted and very clearly say "I don't eat from the trash!" But in a relationship, people don't have the same clear standards. If your partner offers you something that could be potentially unhealthy or downright dangerous you might rationalize it and try to explain why it might be okay to eat some shit. You are more likely to eat shit when you don't love and value yourself.

The absence of self love can cause so many problems in your life. You can get yourself into emotional situations that are hard and sometimes impossible to get out of. When you are vulnerable people can spot it like a bulls eye on your chest and they waste no time in taking advantage of your confusion, sadness, low self-esteem, and innocence. Being a lesbian does not exclude you from encountering assholes. When you love yourself, you can become more aware of the pitfalls of love. Merging your life with anyone is not a small task. You have to examine the good and the bad. So take care of yourself first by loving yourself and then by examining and studying some of the things that can go wrong in a relationship. Love yourself enough to empower yourself.

In the Black lesbian community, intimate partner violence, previously called domestic violence has doubled over the last five years. More and more women are finding themselves staying in physically abusive same-sex relationships. This is astonishing seeing that most people have the notion that women are less violent than men. In general, this increase in intimate violence is due to lesbian studs that believe their role as the "man" in the relationship requires dominance, aggression, and control of the "woman" in the relationship. They are terrorizing their partners. I know that some people may object to this statement, but truth is truth. Lesbians get so entangled into their roles and societal labels, and they like to play out what they think their relationships should be like. Yes, the relationship is turned into a game of sorts. They forget that both people in the relationship are women. This causes issues. Major issues!

Power and control has no gender. When you agree to participate in dominant and passive roleplaying in your relationship, you open the flood gates for abuse to occur. A woman with controlling and/or violent tendencies will try to set up roleplaying in the relationship because it sets the stage for her. When you are not aware of the characteristics of your partner, you can become a victim of same sex violence very quickly without realizing what is happening. And, if you are a woman that is being pressed to hold the dominant position you might fall into the trap of becoming controlling and/or abusive, even if that is not what you set out to do.

Before you get into your next relationship or if you are currently in a relationship, learn about intimate partner violence. Learn the signs, the red flags, and warnings of potential violence. Learn about safety plans and how to get out. Learn where to go for help. More importantly learn how to ASK for help. Remember, you don't really know the person you may fall in love with until time has passed. You need to know what can happen and you need to be able to identify things that may have already happened in your relationship. Know your limits and be clear about your standards. Be clear on what is acceptable and what is not acceptable in your life. Abuse is wrong and it is NEVER your fault if you are being abused. You can empower yourself by learning the signs of an abusive person. If you are always begging for a relationship and not taking time to examine yourself, you can be caught off guard by an abuser.

There are local shelters and organizations in every city that has information on Intimate Partner Violence. The services are free and anonymous. But remember, whether heterosexual or lesbian most victims of abuse are women. This being stated, often times, the shelters could help your abuser or let her into the shelter with you. This is a tactic that lesbians use to keep their control and find their partners. So do not be afraid to admit that your abuser is a woman. Love yourself first. Empower yourself with knowledge!

When you are not in love with yourself you can also become dependent on your partner to make you happy. This is a BIG, HUGE mistake! No one can make you happy, no one. You and only you can create happiness within. You are placing a huge responsibility on your partner and setting your relationship up for disaster. Have you ever seen relationships that seem more like a "Mother/Daughter" relationship instead of a romantic, loving relationship?

During my survey I met a couple from Nevada, Sandy and Tammy. I spent a lot of time interviewing Tammy, who had just recently broke off her relationship with Sandy. It was a hard time for her, but she was willing to talk and give me details of their three year on-again/off-again relationship. Sandy was a clinically depressed woman with several childhood issues. At the beginning of their relationship Tammy had just come out of a tough break-up and was on the cusp of healing from a long-term relationship. It was their individual ordeals that brought them together. Tammy was seeking help from a therapist and trying to move past her hurt but Sandy looked to Tammy and their relationship to heal her. Tammy found herself being a mother, therapist, maid, and financial supporter for Sandy. Sandy wanted Tammy to make her happy. She needed Tammy to help her be happy. Tammy was working diligently to make herself happy and was tired of the responsibility of Sandy. Sandy was not adding to the quality of her life, but taking from it. During one of the tantrums that Sandy often had, Tammy decided to love herself enough to end the relationship. She had had enough. Since that relationship, Sandy has been in two more failed relationships. She still isn't happy. She is still waiting for someone to make her happy. Sandy will never be happy until she makes herself happy.

It is not the job of your loving partner to make you happy. It is not your job to make your partner happy. That is not what relationships are for. When you enter into a relationship and are not clear about your intentions this dependence can happen. Once again GET CLEAR! Don't allow this trap to catch you off guard. Make yourself happy first! Loving yourself allows you to come to the relationship as a whole person.

When you desire a relationship, take your time. The perfect relationship will happen when you both are ready. You have to go through a process for the perfect relationship. Your perfect partner is also going through a process. Just be ready when it happens.

A Healthy Relationship

What is a perfect Black lesbian relationship? "After 30 years, she is still my air. I am so blessed that she is my wife," said a prominent minster from California. When asked what made her relationship sustaining and loving after all those years she simply replied, "Love, my dear, Love."

My wife said of me after two years, "Ray, you are an exquisite symphony. I love you … Still!" We just celebrated our second year of marriage.

"Our love continues to grow and it is wonderful. I love her. No matter what, I love her," said Denise from Chicago.

It seems that deep, true love is the key to a healthy, happy relationship. But, we must examine the word love. In the case of healthy relationships, love is an action word. It is not an adjective that describe how you feel, rather it is a verb that tells us what you do! My wife always tells me to never listen to what she says, but watch what she does. Action is the key to relationships. When you love actively, you do what is in the best interest of your partner. You seek her highest good at all times, and you honor her in your thoughts and with your actions. This means that you don't force her to come out and you don't force her to stay in the closet. You don't expect her to take care of you like your mother and you don't expect her to leave you hanging in times of need. You are nice and kind and pleasant to her. You have empathy for situations that she may be in. You aim to live in your highest self and you self examine enough to try to maintain your mental and emotional health. This is Love!

After becoming clear about who you are and learning to love who you are, there are eight additional things that you can do to find and keep a perfect relationship. Perfection is when you and your partner fit like a puzzle. You may be different, come from different backgrounds, and think differently, but together you're smooth and beautiful. That is perfection.

3. Write a list of your attributes

This will make you clear about the piece of the puzzle you are bringing to the table. List the attributes you currently have that you like and want to keep. List the things about you that you don't like, realistic things you want to work on. This list will be your guide as you are on your journey.

4. Write a list of the attributes you would like in a person

When you are clear-headed and not in the throes of passion with a new love interest, write down what you seek in your perfect partner. This will allow you to be honest with yourself on the type of partner that you truly want. Writing a list gives you the opportunity to choose who you want to date. It is easy to become passive in your quest to date and allow people to choose you. Your list gives you the power and the ability to make the choice for yourself. Writing a list takes away the desperation of finding someone and gives you an opportunity to not settle on one of the most important decisions in your life.

Your list is your roadmap to love. It will guide you to your deep desire and keep you living in truth. Take time daily to look at your list. Examine your list and make changes as you see fit. As you begin to date make sure that the people you give your time and energy have attributes that are on your list. Be consistent and stay on your path. Knowing what you want is the key. If you already have someone you are with, use these steps to evaluate if you should leave or stay. You want to be happy right? Don't trip. Either way re-evaluate this list from time to time. You may have to let go for your perfection to appear.

5. Make sure that both attributes match; equally yoked and balance

You have to be equally yoked! You must be compatible. This applies to you as a Black lesbian, just as it applies to all of your heterosexual friends. Your relationship will blow up if you are not equally yoked. This means that you have to fit. Oil and water do not mix! No matter what they tell you, opposites may attract, but they don't last! You have to have common desires, attractions, goals, beliefs, values, and morals. Your dreams for your lives cannot contradict each other. How you choose to express them may be different, but they have to be there in the first place. If you like a neat house, your partner should like a neat house. If you eat healthy, your partner must like eating healthy. If you believe in a higher power, your partner must believe in a higher power. If you want kids, your partner should want kids; how many, can be up for debate! These similarities must be present BEFORE you meet each other. Changing your partner's cleaning habits, eating habits, and spiritual beliefs to fit yours is not compatibility, its control.

Settling is never an option. Never settle on love and, in your life, never settle for not loving you first. Never compromise your desires. Just remember …some will,… some won't, …so what, … NEXT! Move on in your relationships until you find what you really want. If you have done the first three steps this should not be hard for you to do. The wait will be so worth it! Trust me, I know…

6. Prepare for your partner by becoming mentally, physically, and financially fit

Mental health is important. I know I said it earlier, but it is essential in your relationship. Black lesbians stay together longer than other homosexual relationships, but it is usually out of loyalty, pity, or emotional or financial dependence. Just as in a heterosexual relationship, a mentally ill Black woman will drive you crazy! Don't take that craziness into your relationship. Therapy is good for your soul. While you are working on your mental health, check your physical and financial health. Nobody wants an unhealthy, mentally unstable, and overweight, broke woman. Being a lesbian doesn't give you a license to dress sloppy and be overweight. Go to the gym. Eat healthy. Get your money together. Better yet, save some money. Have something to bring to the table.

7. Don't U-Haul, Commit

U-Hauling is not a wise idea! Good sex doesn't mean you move in immediately, it doesn't even mean the person you had sex with is relationship material. It's just an orgasm for goodness sake! When you move in with a person before you get a chance to know them, you are asking for trouble. Honor yourself. Honor your relationship. Make sure that you live alone for some time. When you can be by yourself, you know that you are ready to be with someone else. U-hauling makes lesbians look silly and sometimes desperate to each other and everybody else. The relationship usually doesn't last more than six months and you are off to the next one. A long lasting relationship takes time to build and is worth its weight in solid foundation. Society and families will never take you seriously if you don't take yourself seriously. Relationships are the key indicator to your family that you are truly a lesbian. The first real relationship to show off is the one to yourself. Before you enter into a relationship, Black families think you are confused and God will come and deliver you. When you get into a serious relationship with yourself and the realization that you have accepted being lesbian, they are forced to accept you for who you are. This is your chance to live with integrity and show them that you are CLEAR about who you are. If you jump into a serious relationship with the first woman you sleep with, then they will just think that you are a whore and loose; just as they would if you were in a heterosexual relationship. Same sex, same problems. Seek a deserving partner and build your relationship before loading up the U-Haul and moving in. Build yourself and your relationship before reintroducing yourself and her to your family. If you can't afford to live alone and pay your bills then you have no business getting into a relationship. You still have work to do!

At the other end of the spectrum from U-Hauling are those who don't commit. You know who you are. You say you are in love, you are in relationships for many years, but you don't take any steps to solidify your relationship. You cannot have a healthy relationship if you do not really commit to each other. In many states lesbians do not have the option to marry legally. That does not mean you cannot have a ceremony to communicate to your friends, family, and the world that you are committed to each other and you are building a life together. Having a ceremony tells everyone, including yourselves "we are serious". You will feel like a married couple and you will act accordingly.

If you determine a ceremony is not right for you, commit to each other through documentation. Even if you do have a ceremony, it is very important to back it up with legal documentation. Take steps to merge into a unit rather than two separate entities. Put her name on the lease or the deed to the house. Make at least one of your bank accounts a joint account. Draw up your will, medical durable power of attorney, and financial power of attorney. A will describes who you want to care for your children and pets and what you want to happen with your property when you pass away. With a medical power of attorney you give your partner the authority to make medical decisions for you if you are not able to make these decisions yourself. A financial power of attorney gives her the authority to make financial decisions for you if you are not able to make these decisions for yourself. If you have a strong aversion to putting your partner's name on the lease or you do not feel comfortable naming your partner in your will or making her responsible for making medical and financial decisions for you then that's a HUGE clue that she is not the one you should be with. Go back to steps 4 and

5 to get clear on what you are looking for and determining compatibility.

8. Romance Her Always

Romance is the sweetness in your relationship. Without it your relationship is without passion. And without passion, the relationship is just merely a friendship. You are a lesbian, so be a lesbian and love her slowly, softly, and gently. Romance is the spice that keeps it tasting good.

My wife and I have had a date every Friday night for the last four years. We haven't missed a Friday date night yet. No matter how tiring or frustrating work was, we take the time to love on each other. Embrace the good and the bad. Our date begins from the moment that we get off of work. The cell phones go off, and we go and get sexy for each other. We either plan our dates together or one of us plans something for us to do together. Our date may be at home or out on the town. But it is always with just the two of us. This is not the day for excuses on why you can't be with your wife or partner. This is the day that is all about you and why you two decided to become one in the first place. My Friday date nights are marvelous. I mean spectacular!

Join us and set up a date night that happens every week. On your date focus on each other. No matter how long you have been with each other, give each other quality time. Read the book *The Five Love Languages* by Gary Chapman. Find out how your partner receives and gives love. Discuss your love languages. Learn how to grow in your weaknesses and build on your strengths. Learn how to love yourself and your partner.

If you and your partner have problems spending hours at a time together without disagreements or boredom, you might need to re-examine your relationship. Go back to Steps 1 and 2. Do either of you have unresolved issues that you brought into the relationship such as low self-esteem, inadequate finances, baby-Daddy drama? Do you as a couple have unresolved issues such as infidelity? If you do not want to spend uninterrupted time together because of boredom go back to Step 5. Do you match? Do you have shared interests? Are you compatible?

9. Support her — Throw control out the window

Control is so old. Throw it out the window. Learn how to accept and support your partner. You can't control anything but yourself. You can't make anyone do anything. You can't make your partner love you the way you want to be loved. If you are not happy, then leave or don't pursue a relationship. But do not try to control your partner. This will lead to each of your demise. There is a subtle blessing in accepting your partner for who they are. This is how you get to know them like no one else does. Acceptance leads to unconditional love. The same is true for you. Accept yourself for who you are and you will unconditionally love yourself. This is when your relationship moves into forever.

This ninth step is so important for the long haul of your relationship. Without it you shouldn't get married, move in with each other, or try to be committed. Merging as one is a result of acceptance. You both become so comfortable and okay with whom each other is that you become and live out the oneness in your lives together.

10. Always Start Back at One!

What is one? It is what you did when you first laid eyes on her. The thing that made your eyes sparkle. You know those things like the poems, the love cards, the understanding, the patience, and the tenderness that you gave when you were courting her. Continue to be transparent, willing, and open. Polish your jewel, appreciate your jewel, and more importantly massage your jewel. The beginning is a wonderful thing. The middle is always in need of some work and the end result is happiness all the time even when there are moments of questioning. This is the time to go back! Every day of your relationship, remember what you did and how you felt when she first entered into your life. Remember what made you smile and what you did to make her smile. Remember the butterflies in your stomach. Every day, all day, remember.

These steps will lead you to a happy, satisfied, healthy relationship. With society, families, and religious organizations against us, we must establish relationships that breed life. As a Black lesbian, you are faced with so many challenges because you are Black, because you are a woman, and because you are same gender loving. Learn to create a paradise inside yourself and within your home so that you can love "IT" as well!

10 Steps to a Healthy Relationship

1. Get clear about who you are!

2. Value yourself

3. Write a list of your attributes

4. Write a list of the attributes you would like in a person

5. Make sure that both attributes match; equally yoked and balance

6. Prepare for your partner by becoming mentally, physically, and financially fit

7. Don't U-Haul, Commit

8. Romance her always

9. Support her—Throw control out the window

10. Always start back at One!

CHAPTER 7

CHILDREN

S aying that children are important to women is an understatement. Many Black lesbians have children. Being a lesbian does not silence your biological clock. In fact, if you are in a healthy, loving relationship, your home might be the perfect place to raise children. If you do not yet have children, know that you are not precluded from having children. You may carry and birth a child conceived with a sperm donor. Children may enter your life through your partner or adoption. Children may also come into your life through family relationships and mentor programs. The reality and thought of children in your life can create challenges for single lesbians and lesbian couples. In this chapter, I want to communicate to you that if you are open and intentional children can be a positive part of you being same gender loving and loving it.

If you are in a relationship, there may be one woman who really wants to have a child and another woman who wouldn't mind not having a child. What happens when you both want children and you begin to look at your options: sperm bank, live donor, or adoption? What about the baby's daddy? What do your children call your wife/partner? When and how should you come out to your children? How do you deal with discrimination toward you and your children? It becomes complicated, doesn't it? These questions are real and you will face them as a lesbian if you have or plan to have children in your life.

The Child's Eyes

I want to take a moment for you to look at this situation from a child's point of view. Growing up in America as a Black child is not an easy measure. Yes, times are getting better, but the issues that stem from being Black in America are still prevalent in our daily lives. Your child has these issues to contend with as well as having two Mommies. If both of their Mommies are unhealthy they have already lost the game of life. So once again you loving "IT", who you are, is important and vital to your life. When you have children, loving who you are becomes important and vital to their lives as well.

Coming Out to Your Child

First off, DO NOT LIE TO YOUR CHILD ABOUT WHO YOU ARE! This includes lying by omission. Do not keep silent about your lesbianism and wait for your child to figure it out or ask you about it. That might make you more comfortable but it will mean a lot of confusion for your child. It begins with you. If you start out by lying to your child, you have taught your child that you are ashamed to be a lesbian. Don't do that. Your partner is not their Aunt, God Mom, or friend. They are the potential parent to your child. Anything else is a lie and you are feeding into the societal status quo! GET CLEAR and BE CLEAR about the relationship you have with your child(ren) before you bring someone into their lives and before you decide to have children. It all starts with you. If you come out later in your life, tell your child(ren) as soon as possible. Don't lie to them. They deserve to hear it from you!

Here are some examples of ways to tell your children you are a lesbian.

> *"Sweetie, some girls date boys, some girls date girls, and some boys date boys. I'm a girl that dates girls. I didn't tell you before because I was waiting for you to be old enough to understand. Do you have any questions for me?"*

For an older child or adult child:

"I want to tell you something about myself that I was afraid to talk to you about before. I was afraid you might stop loving me if you knew that I prefer to date and be in relationships with other women. I am a lesbian. I'm telling you now because I think it's important to the health of our family for you to know. Do you have any questions for me?"

It is important to ask your children if they have questions and it is important that you listen and answer their questions as honestly as possible. When you discuss your lesbianism with your children your common themes should be: there is nothing wrong with being a lesbian and you are happy to be who you are, and they, as a separate and distinct being are free to feel however they feel about you being a lesbian. You do not need to try to control your children's feelings on this issue, you just have to be honest and try to model self-love and self-acceptance for them.

Your Child and Your Family

Your family can also be a challenge for your child. If you already have a child or children, your family will tend to embrace the child and exclude your partner in every way possible. They won't acknowledge her and often times will talk bad about her to your child. They might even condemn your lesbianism in front of your child. Your family can put a wedge between you, your child(ren), and the relationship that you are trying to establish with your partner.

Despite your family's behavior, you might keep taking your child around your family for several good reasons. You might need help with childcare or maybe you don't want to deprive your child the joy of spending time with grandparents, aunts, uncles, and cousins. So, how do you include your family in your child's life while protecting your child's and your own mental health?

Sharon, from Tennessee, talks frankly about the challenges in her life involving her child and family. "I remember, when I decided to 'come out' to my family. The first thing they said is 'Don't take Jaizon around that sinful mess'. They refused to acknowledge me as a lesbian and they shunned any woman I ever brought home. My son, Jaizon was 6 years old, and was able to notice how they were treating me in his presence. When I finally got into a serious relationship, they tried to convince my son that he should stay with them for good. All of a sudden my son starting acting out and begging to go to my parents house. He hated my girlfriend without cause. It was horrible. My relationship ended, and to this day, I live alone with just my son so that I won't be at risk of losing him ever again."

I am saddened by Sharon's situation. I am saddened that her family caused so much pain to such a wonderful lady. This challenge is one that is all too familiar for so many. Black parents have no idea the amount of hurt they cause their children and grandchildren. As a Black lesbian, trying to extend your immediate family can be costly. But if you have courage to get through the hell that your family brings you, the rest of society is easy. Nothing will be as bad for you and your child as your family.

There is No Lesbian-Friendly Bubble

Outside of your family you and your child will have to deal with the community at large. There are the dreaded children at school and in the neighborhood, and the dreaded parents of those dreadful children. There are plenty of parents out there telling their children that being gay is a sin. They are not teaching love and tolerance. You and your child will encounter them and their offspring. Some other hurdles can include schools, physician offices, hospitals, social clubs and children's activities such as sports and boy scouts. If you choose a private school or religious school for your child, the administration can be prejudiced and make it difficult for your partner to be involved with your child's schooling. Hospitals and doctor's offices can be accepting or rejecting depending on the staff. Religious organizations can be belittling depending on who you are affiliated with and where you attend.

You cannot raise your children in a lesbian-friendly bubble but you can limit their exposure to people that do not love and accept who you are and the dynamics of your family. It is not worth the mental and internal damage that they will cause your child. True, there will be situations that are totally unavoidable. You both will have to deal with jerks and assholes. Having two mommies isn't quite popular and bullying hasn't gone away, it has become worse. Having two mommies is fuel, precious fuel for bullies. Any parent knows that it is not your job to eliminate all challenges that your child could face. That is a sure fire way to emotionally cripple your child. It is your job to prepare them and equip them with tools to overcome the challenges they face.

School

When you have school aged children, it would be best to establish a relationship with the teacher, principal, and staff of your child. Be persistent at getting to know some of the parents of your child's friends. Stay active and involved. Be open about being a lesbian while you are getting to know people. People hate what they don't know. So let them get to know you and your family. Introduce your partner and explain that she is your child's other parent. You will be surprised at how many people are accepting when they get to know you.

When you encounter prejudice, stand up and speak out. Your children are watching you. They are learning how to deal with these situations from watching how you deal with them. Bullying exists. Later, I will discuss the bullying that happens with our teens that are lesbian but children of lesbians are bullied as well. As a parent, it is your job to decrease and stop bullying from happening to your child. The first lesson that you should teach your child is, "everyone is not your friend." Your child needs to learn early on that there are some mean, bad people in the world. They need to know that every child or classmate that they encounter will not necessarily like them or accept their two mommies or their lesbian mom. If they learn this lesson early on in their development, your child(ren) won't be disappointed when it happens. They will be able to bounce back quicker than if they were not aware.

The next lesson that you need to teach your child, is "seeking help is a cool thing". They are not punks for telling, or snitching on people who hurt them. They need to learn that no one has the right to treat them bad. Bullies often times get away with bullying because their victims stay quiet. Let your child's teacher and principal know that you will not tolerate your child being bullied because of who you are. Know your rights and exercise them if you need to.

The last lesson that you should teach your child is "shame is not allowed." Let them know that you are proud of who you are. Who you are is normal and right. Let go of the internal homophobia so that your child can stand proud of who you are as well. This becomes important in how your child reacts to the bullying. They have to be proud to stand up for their family. If you don't teach your son to be proud, then he will buy into the lie that there is something wrong with you and your family. Banish shame from your life and teach your child(ren) not to ever let it into their hearts.

If you prepare your children properly for school and for bullying, the process may go more smoothly than you imagined. It is important that you take the time early on to give your child all of the necessary tools to survive. Remember, they didn't ask to be here. You brought them into this world, so take care of them. Protect their innocence. It's your job and their right!

What About the "Baby Daddy"?

Yep, he still exists even though you are a lesbian. Your child has a father. He or she could not exist without having a biological mother AND father. Since this is a fact, it is inappropriate for you to ever say your child does not have a father. Studies show that most Black lesbians conceive their child naturally before 'coming out.' Very few adopt and very few use a sperm donor to have a child. With this being said, there is usually a baby daddy lurking in your life.

I have struggled with the Baby Daddy issue when deciding whether to have children. My wife is not a man and can never be a father to our children. I am not asking her to be a father. We are two same gender, loving women who wish to have children one day. As a teacher and a child advocate, I witness several children try to cope without having a father in their lives. They are confused and hurt as to why their fathers don't want them or love them. As Black lesbians, we can only do our best. We don't have the traditional nuclear family, but our children do deserve to have a father in their lives if possible. So, let's stop the games. Get over yourself and what works best for you. Don't get pregnant on purpose and lie to the daddy about your sexual orientation. Don't shut your child's father out of his or her life. Don't tell your children that your partner is the only daddy they need. That's just wrong.

Tameka, from Georgia, dated Jason until she got pregnant. She knew that she was a lesbian, but really wanted a child. So she acted like she was in love with Jason. He was clueless. Once she got pregnant, she dumped him and told him she was a lesbian. Jason was crushed. It was nothing but grace and the baby that kept him from strangling her. Once the baby was born, she put him through hell to even see the child. She and her lesbian partner had decided that Jason should not be involved in the child's life. Jason eventually went to court to fight for custody rights and got them. What Tameka did is not the way to extend your family. The consequences of her action put her child through the ringer. Every child deserves to have their father in their lives. If your child's father is abusive or neglectful then, of course, you should not put your child at risk. But, even in that case, your child at least deserves to know who his or her father is.

If you are one of the few that decides to adopt or go the sperm bank route to have children, having a male role model in your child's life is key. A God Father or uncle would be great for your child. Male energy is important and creates balance in the lives of children. Men see the world and walk through the world differently than women. Men can model behaviors that you want your child to learn. Just because you are a lesbian doesn't mean that you shouldn't have male energy in your life. And having a man or men in your life does not mean you need to look at them in a sexual way. Again, males are important to provide balance. Balance is important to maintain the order of life and peace comes from balance. So strengthen the relationships with the positive men in your life or try to establish positive, non-sexual relationships with the men in your life before you think about having children. If you already have children, start working on this right away. Your child will thank you later!

CHAPTER 8

TEENS

I t is important that you (Adults) take the time to think about all of the young, teenage Black lesbians. If you are the parent of a lesbian teen or young adult you must educate yourself on the specific issues they will face because of their youth. They are our future and our legacy. You must protect their spirits, their hopes, and their dreams.

It is no secret that society makes being who we are difficult at times. Teenage lesbians are more courageous than we ever were in middle and high school. Thus, they are more scrutinized than we ever were in middle and high school. I have talked to several teens and they wanted their voices to be heard about love, bullying, family, and life. Before I address teens directly, I want to share some of their stories in their words.

Joi, 13 years old… "I don't know why I just can't be myself. I'm sick of it." Joi was referring to the students in her school that taunted her to change her clothes because she was dressed in boy clothes. Joi changed her shirt and pants to more form fitting clothes and took off her ball cap . In tears she said, "I don't like boys. I like girls and I like dressing this way. No one understands me. I have the same feeling as everyone else, I just like girls instead." Her school was Christian-based and the staff didn't do much to solve Joi's dilemma. The teachers and staff believed Joi could solve her own problem by not dressing and acting the way she did. They also believed she was too young to make permanent decisions and declarations about her sexual identity. Joi just continued to suffer in silence. She has already attempted suicide twice.

Alicia, 16 years old said, "I know that I am not like other girls. But I don't feel like I am wrong or bad. I'm just different. I have the most resistance to who I am in my family. My father is a minister at my church but, it is my mother that pressures me to 'act like a lady'. My father doesn't say much, he just sits back and looks on. But I can tell he disapproves of me. My mother nags me daily, to get a boyfriend, to wear dresses, to be like my sisters. I try to tell her, it ain't gonna happen, but she just nags harder. She doesn't realize that I just shut down and keep the most intimate details about myself to myself. I feel like a stranger in my own home. I'm the middle child and my older sister is in college and my younger sister is still in elementary school. So I usually try not to even come out of my room.

I have tried to be with guys. Really I have. I have prayed and prayed for God to make me not be gay. But nothing ever changes. The more I resisted being a lesbian, the more I felt like a lesbian. I don't really trust God because everyone in church says that God is love, but God doesn't love me. According to them, I'm a sinner. I don't want to think about going to hell so I just stay away from God.

I have a girlfriend that I have been dating for about a year. She is wonderful and she makes me so happy. We are like secret lovers though. Her family is cool and they love me. They support us, but no one in my family even knows she exists. She is just my secret. I keep it like that because I don't want my mother to take this happiness from me. I don't want my relationship to become tainted with fights. It sucks, but it's my life."

Candyce, 14 years old… "I don't really care what people say about me. I am a lesbian and I love myself. I don't try to be like them or what my family wants me to be. It's my life. I guess I am rebellious, but really I don't care. I mean, look at me. Does it look like I want to be with a boy? People just think about who I might be kissing or who I want to date, but no one ever ask me if dating wasn't an option what I would do. I would still be a lesbian because it is not about who I want to kiss or date. This is about who I am on the inside. Sexuality is just seen when I choose to kiss someone. I have been like this my entire life."

Tammi, 20 year old college student... "I have always been the good child. My parents relied on me to be responsible and help out with my younger siblings. I am smart, funny and loving, and a lesbian. My parents didn't know all of me and once I left for college I thought that it would be better if they never knew. College opened up my world! I took a women's studies class that taught me ideas and concepts that freed me from my inner bondage. I wanted a real relationship with my parents so I decided at winter break I would tell them who I really was. I knew that my parents wouldn't be completely accepting, but I had no idea they would disown me. They no longer wanted to be a part of my life. They even stopped paying for college. My mother would not even talk to me. I felt like I might give in to their pressure but then I found a church that accepted me and began to receive love from the congregation. I know I am not wrong for being who I am, but I am so hurt though, and at times my church family simply isn't enough. I hate it that people think that anyone would ever choose this."

Jamie, a 24 year old graduate student... "My depression runs deep in my soul. It is like a dagger that stabs my heart on a continuous basis. I sometimes find solace and comfort in God. My church is amazing and I have a new love in my life. Sometimes the pain is lifted by the warmth that surrounds me, but I never feel free. I just wish my Daddy still loved me. Why does it matter that I am a lesbian? Why does it matter that I am in love with a woman? Why isn't my smile, my intelligence, my zeal enough to be wanted by the ones that gave me life? I just want to be free and to truly be me. I don't think anyone really understands me. People listen and are around, but they don't really get me. I wish I can be more than just a Black lesbian in the eyes of this world, but the reality is, I'm not. So maybe the depression will win after all."

Jamie committed suicide and left a raging hole in the lives of all who knew and loved her in 2009.

If you are a teen/young adult, your voice has been heard. Your voice is being heard as you tread through your journey. For many of you, your struggles and concerns are the same as mentioned in the previous chapters of this book. But it is also evident that you deal with different elements and circumstances as a Black teen/young adult lesbian. It is much harder for you to experience love and to use your voice because you are still dependent on the adults in your life. Your stakes are so much higher when you come out and begin to accept who you are as a lesbian. The Black community does not provide you sympathy or grace simply because you are still a child. They don't care how old you are. And this is the reality that you live day after day.

As someone who is same gender loving and loving it, I offer you these words of encouragement, support, and direction as you continue your journey. And I plead with every woman who is same gender loving and loving it to embrace our youth, stand up for our youth, and be for them what you wished someone would have been for you.

Young Love!

Okay, now I know that you have the love bug like every other person in our society, and that is cool. Love is a beautiful thing when it is right and healthy. Yet, I know you are probably thinking, "Why is it so hard to find love and keep it?" As a teen/young adult, navigating through your love situations can be truly difficult. The first thing you wonder is, "How do I know if the girl I like is a lesbian?" You may have problems on how to approach someone you like. You may be scared. So here is a little advice when it comes to love.

First, focusing on love at your age can impede your goals. So before you are ready to give your all to someone else, make sure you have given your all to yourself. Remember that you are a lesbian and when emotions start to fly high, your world can become a whirlwind. So make sure that you are progressing in your life at the rate and speed that you desire before you begin to spread yourself around.

Second, the best way to find love is to get busy doing things that you love with people who are like you. There are several lesbian youth groups, clubs, and activities you can get involved with in your community. This will decrease some anxiety you have about hanging around people who are not like you. You can be comfortable if you choose to ask someone out on a date. Make sure that you keep your time with anyone fun and light. You have the rest of your life to be serious and "play house".

Finally, surround yourself and your girlfriend with older healthy Black lesbian couples. Find a mentor that can guide you and be a support system to you in your relationships. As a Black lesbian teen/young adult, many times you don't have anyone to talk to about relationship stuff. Heterosexual friends don't get it and the adults in your life don't acknowledge it as a "real" relationship. So make sure you grab hold of individuals that will validate your relationship. It is important.

Dating and interacting at your age may be difficult, but it is possible. You can have the same childhood as your heterosexual friends. Your future can be the same as any heterosexual person in America. You can get a great education, work at a great job, and have loving and supportive friends. You can have the wedding of your dreams, have children, live in the house you want, and enjoy all of the liberties that come with being a "couple". You may have to work harder at it or fill out additional paperwork, or work up enough courage to follow your dreams, but it can happen. Your future is bright and you can have anything that you want.

Trust me, I know. I had the biggest wedding ever in a Black church in a state that has a constitutional amendment prohibiting same-sex marriage. I had over 125 people attend my wedding and it was the best day of my life. My wife is worth all of the pain I ever endured. You can be happy and it does get better. Go for it!

Bullies

Bullying and teasing have always been a part of the teenage culture, but it has never been as torturous as it is today. With the rapid growth of technology and social networking, bullying can now occur 24 hours a day, 7 days a week. Bullying has now taken on an ugly face that can lead to severe consequences for the victim. As a Black lesbian teen/young adult, you can become a target for such bullying. Being bullied can impede your coming out process, lower your self esteem, cause you to develop depression, and make you want to drop out of school. You must understand bullies and why they do what they do so that you will realize their behavior is not really about you.

There are many causes to bullying that has nothing to do with you. Low self-esteem, jealousy, peer pressure, repeating of behavior, power, and control are some causes that lead people to want to begin bullying. It is their own internal conflict that leads them to begin picking with you. So stop thinking that you have done something wrong or you need to change something about you to be accepted. If you were not a lesbian they would likely find something else about you and bully you for that reason. A bully needs psychological help. They pick on you because they hate themselves.

People bully because they see others doing it, they want to hang out with the right crowd, it makes them feel stronger, smarter, or better than the person they are bullying, and because it's one of the best ways to keep others from bullying them. Once again, it is not because of you!

The best way to deal with a bully is to stay calm and alert. Consider the options and do nothing to escalate the situation. Walk away. Fighting isn't worth it. You do not have to prove yourself by fighting. Take a non-violent stand. Speak respectfully: "I don't want to fight you." Report the bully to authorities, but make sure to discuss with the authorities how you will be protected from retaliation. Find safety or call for help. It is the responsibility of your parents, teachers, coaches, mentors to stop bullying. But you must report it. Bullying won't stop if no one knows about it.

As a Black teen/young adult lesbian, you have to be prepared for bullying. Being and expressing who you really are is easier said than done when you know that the consequence could lead to bullying. But if you know your worth and equip yourself with earlier tools discussed, you can overcome bullying and get on to loving who you are.

Family

As a young person your family is the center of your life. Your mother, father, grandparents, aunts, uncles, and cousins are your base as you grow into adulthood. They are the ones that have taught you about life. So I know that it is heartbreaking that some of your family do not accept who you are. This must be a frightening place to be in your life, especially if you are financially dependent on them or still in high school. Losing their support can mean losing your home and your future dreams and goals.

When dealing with your family, I am going to suggest that you use your best judgment. You are the only one that has to deal with your consequences so make sure that whatever you do, you are ready. My cousin says, "Don't get mad, get what you want." So keep in mind what you want and need and make sure you are doing what you can to get it. That means if you are in your senior year of high school and your mother says she will put you out of the house if you continue to date girls, consider complying with her demands so that you can stay put and finish school. Once you are in college, you can do what you want. If you are in college and you are not sure if your parents will continue to pay for your education if you come out, maybe coming out to them is not necessary at this time. At least not until you have secured alternate ways to fund your education. Be smart, be your first advocate and your own protector. Take care of you!

If your blood family just won't support you, love you, and treat you well, then go and create a village of loving friends and mentors that will have your back. You can't change your family, but you can create the life you desire and friendships that will enhance your life.

CHAPTER 9

THE BLACK LESBIAN COMMUNITY

A house divided will always fall to its death. The community of Black lesbians is a powerful, collective source of resilient women. But Black lesbians are women first and women are raised and socialized to compete with each other. Because of this socialization, all women have the capacity to be "mean girls" to some extent. Jealousy, back-biting, and gossip keep us from giving each other the love and support we need to face the challenges that society creates for us.

If you are serious about being same gender loving and loving "IT", you have to become a safe haven for Black lesbians everywhere. Having your own individual issues and challenges does not excuse how you act toward your lesbian sister. There are so many people suffering because of the cruel behavior of the world around them, they do not need to suffer because of you. Your sisterly love can be the gateway for so many Black lesbians to embrace themselves. Your actions can lead to the reaction of women in your circle and cause either a positive or negative effect. If you have your 'stuff' together, then take the time to help someone else get their 'stuff' together.

You can be your own worst enemy. You can also be the enemy of the community when you do not show love. When you think about where you are in your life and where you want to be, do you ever think about what is stopping you from getting there? There are many things that may have happened in your life that was not in your control. Some people may have hurt you, left you, and abandoned you. You may have mental or physical complications that you were born with. Your parents may not have been the best example in your life. The quality of your education may have been sub-standard. You may have grown up poor and so on. But, those things and people are not always what stop you from living your best life. Those things are not always your enemy. It is not your circumstances that keep you in turmoil. It is you. You are the one that is holding yourself back. Your dreams, your realities, and your desires are now in your control. It is not the responsibility of the world to make you happy. You must make you happy. Every choice that you make has a direct consequence that can lead to your happiness or your misery. Yes, there are tools that you need to have in order to create the life that you want, but the power lies within you. Accessing the tools is obtainable. You just need to get out of your own way and make the choice to go for the life that you want.

You are your worst enemy when you feed your mind with negative thoughts. You are your worst enemy when you go around people that are mean and cruel. You are your worst enemy when don't always take care of your physical health. You are your worst enemy when you allow fear to keep you in a life that you hate. It is not your parents, society, your job, or your family that keeps you trapped in the cage of misery. It is you. And when you are your own enemy, you are also the enemy of the Black lesbian community.

You reproduce whether you want to or not. The reproduction becomes what society sees about you and all those you represent. As a community you must be accountable for yourself as well as each other. The first thing you can do to help your community grow strong and become one is stop sleeping with each other's girlfriends. This brings division and keeps animosity going between women. There are plenty of women to go around. The consequences of stealing or sleeping with another person's partner are detrimental. So stop it.

The next thing you can do is to stop gossiping about each other. Gossip is the seed of turmoil. Stay out of people's business if it doesn't concern you. I know that the urge is there to go and tell your friend what you heard about someone else, but it keeps the community divided. It is hard to really like someone when you learned about them from someone else. People's opinions and thoughts about someone can cloud your judgment before you get a chance to know them. Often times, women are bitter because of a bad break up and they spout off horrible things about people that are not necessarily true. When you listen to the gossip, you participate in tearing down another person's character without knowing the entire truth. This leads to community chaos. How can you be a strong united community when you tear each other down?

Because the Black lesbian community is small, it is important that you are friendly with each other. It is also important that you embrace one another and do your best to become friends. Building an alliance with one another is your best defense as a Black lesbian.

A positive thing you can do is create support groups for people in your community. This fosters trust and creates a safe space for Black lesbians in your community. When their parents and religious community rejects them, you can embrace them. You can bring valuable resources to the groups and expose them to the organizations in your area that would support them.

You can also foster a healthy community by changing your individual perspective of what a Black lesbian is. Black lesbians exist on a spectrum and can be described in so many ways. Everyone's relationship, coming out experience, family structure, religious affiliation, etc. does not have to be like yours. How you live out the fabric of your being is particular to you. Stop judging people's experience. You may find that you actually like them.

Your Gay Brothers

The relationship with Black lesbians and Black gay men is complicated and intricate. Although you are both same gender loving, your challenges are very different. Men are socialized to be in charge, never show emotion, take care of their family, produce children, make money, and protect their family. Black men have societal pressures that are designed to make their paths excruciating. Black gay men are hated beyond belief and are not as accepted as their lesbian sisters. Their road is much more difficult.

This difference can cause a strain between you and your gay brothers. Resentment can fester in men because the lesbian plight is not as difficult. Lesbians can be insensitive to the journey of gay men which can cause them to not want to be around lesbians. It is not easy for either of you, but it is extremely hard for Black gay men. As a lesbian, you must be aware of their struggle and respect their struggle. The Black community takes so much longer to accept them. Your understanding and friendship can be the gift they need to keep going.

Another cause for strain can be the gender roles that both of you have been taught. Men and women have ideals of how each other are supposed to act. This causes friction when gay men "act like women" and lesbians "act like men". It is important to remember that both perceptions are wrong and there is no right way to be a woman or a man. But because of socialization, you can be guilty of this association. It creates an unspoken divide that lingers between gay men and lesbians. You must keep in mind that you are both same gender loving and you are both trying to reach the same goal of loving "IT".

There are relationships among gay men and lesbians that are wonderful and great. You may be someone that has broken the barrier that keeps lesbians apart from gay men. That is the goal. As a community, the barriers must be torn down with compassion and understanding. The fight for acceptance and justice is the same for gay men and lesbians. Nothing is more important! Together, you can build a bridge and become one voice. Together, you can be "IT"!

CHAPTER 10

LOVING 'IT'

Reflection can be a very powerful tool in your life. Often, I have reminisced on the times in my life when I always wanted something different than what I had. I wanted a different mother and a different family. I wanted to live in a different state, have a different job, and date someone different. There were times when I wanted a different religion, a different sexuality, and a different life. I went searching and running tying to find the grass that would be greener in my life. I never found the greener grass and I was never content or happy. As a matter of fact, my own grass got brown and ugly!

After time passed, I realized that the life that I have is the perfect life for me. It fits my soul and allows me to breathe in the many blessings and breathe out the many lessons in my life. My life is filled with the right people for the right lessons at the right time. There is nothing better for me.

Taking the time to breathe in your life, and accept the joys and challenges that it has brought you, give you the opportunity to fully enjoy the gift that you are in this world. When you are always looking for something more, something better, you miss the opportunity to be fully present in the life that you have been given. You cannot measure your path by someone else's path. You are on your path for a reason and that reason will lead to your greatness. Embrace your life. All of it! When you accept your path, you are one step closer to your purpose. And your purpose is the greener grass that is awaiting you!

Loving "IT" allows you to bask in the glory of the best of you. You rock! You are so special and needed in the world. Being your best is your gift to yourself. You deserve to experience your best self. Imagine your world when you are living your best life. I bet you can visualize the beauty and joy you can create when you are your best. Become one with your best!

Loving "IT" is also about you continuously doing the work. The work involves: being true to yourself, learning to love yourself, taking care of yourself, protecting and making wise decisions for your children, standing up for who you are, being involved in healthy intimate partner relationships, surrounding yourself with healthy and loving friends and family members, seeking out God for yourself, and living your truth.

As a Black lesbian there are many complexities that make up who you are. Your existence and survival is a blessing in our world and it is necessary for you to preserve your inner most being by taking care of yourself. When you are healthy and in love with yourself, you can help the community be healthy. People will ultimately treat you the way you treat yourself. When you love "IT", people will love you! They will be attracted to your light. The Black lesbian community has so much to offer the world. It is possible for all of us to be Same Gender Loving and Love "IT"!

www.ingramcontent.com/pod-product-compliance
Lightning Source LLC
Chambersburg PA
CBHW071140090426
42736CB00012B/2185